ALL ABOUT SPACE STATIONS

Miriam Gross

PowerKiDS
press.

New York

Published in 2009 by The Rosen Publishing Group, Inc.
29 East 21st Street, New York, NY 10010

Copyright © 2009 by The Rosen Publishing Group, Inc.

First Edition

Editor: Joanne Randolph
Book Design: Greg Tucker
Photo Researcher: Jessica Gerweck

Photo Credits: Cover © Time & Life Pictures/Getty Images; pp. 5, 9, 15, 17, 21 © Getty Images; p. 7 © spacephotos.com/Age Fotostock; p. 11 Photodisc; p. 13 by NASA; p. 19 © National Geographic/Getty Images.

Library of Congress Cataloging-in-Publication Data

Gross, Miriam.
  All about space stations / Miriam Gross. — 1st ed.
      p. cm. — (Blast off!)
  Includes index.
  ISBN 978-1-4358-2737-0 (library binding) — ISBN 978-1-4358-3135-3 (pbk.)
ISBN 978-1-4358-3141-4 (6-pack)
  1. Space stations—Juvenile literature. I. Title.
  TL797.15.G66 2009
  629.44'2—dc22
                                        2008028354

Manufactured in the United States of America
CPSIA Compliance Information: Batch #211370PK: For Further Information Contact Rosen Publishing, New York, New York at 1-800-237-9932

CONTENTS

Have you ever dreamed of visiting space or even of living there? Can you imagine going to sleep and waking up there? Can you imagine working 300 miles (483 km) above Earth? You can do all this and more in a space station.

A space station is a **satellite** where people stay in space for a long time. It orbits, or flies around, Earth. It has places for **astronauts** to sleep and cook food and places to do science **experiments**. You can learn a lot about space by living there!

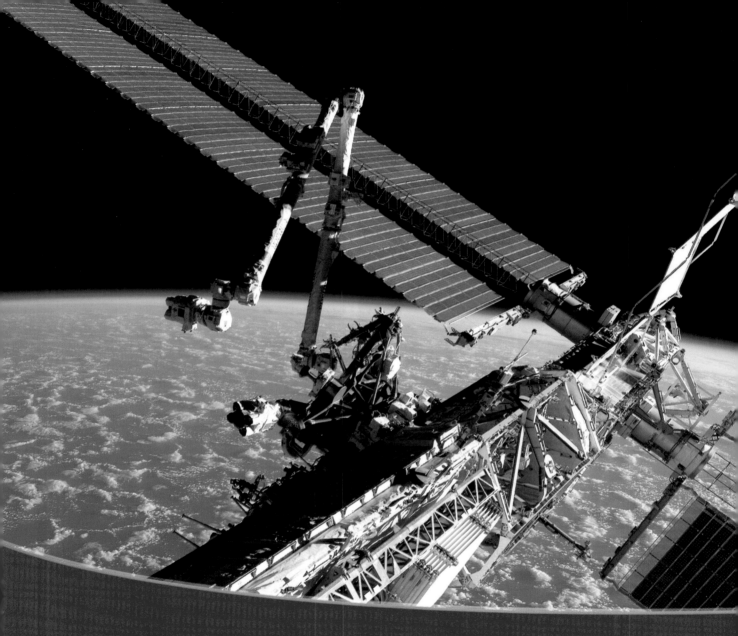

Here is the world's largest space station, called the ISS, as it looked in 2007. The big, flat pieces are solar panels, which use sunlight to power the station.

People began to plan space stations even before the first space rockets were invented. In 1878, a Russian scientist named Konstantin Tsiolkovsky began drawing up plans for a wheel-shaped space station that could orbit Earth.

The first real space station was called *Salyut 1*. It was **launched** by the **Soviet Union** on April 19, 1971. The first attempt to send people to the station failed. The second **mission** was successful. Sadly, though, this second crew died on their way back to Earth. On October 11, 1971, the Soviet Union brought *Salyut 1* back to Earth and destroyed it.

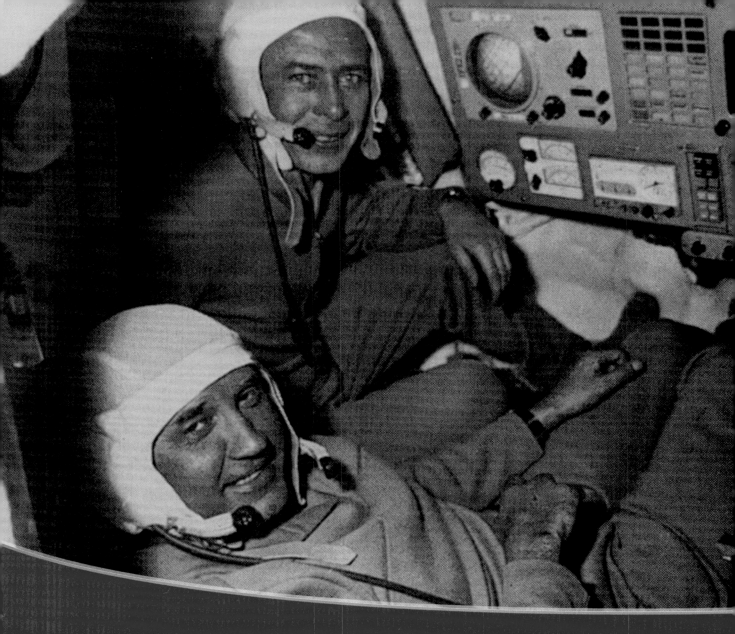

These Soviet cosmonauts are in a Soyuz spacecraft. These spacecraft were used to carry cosmonauts to *Salyut 1*.

1

Space stations are made up of many parts. The core, or central part, of the space station is launched first. The core has docking ports on it. Docking ports are special doorways where spacecraft can connect to the space station and form a tight seal. This allows the crew to safely move from the spacecraft to the space station without getting sucked into space.

Docking ports can also be used to fix new parts to the station. The new parts are called modules. A module might be a **laboratory**, or it could be a place where the astronauts sleep.

This photo shows the docking port on *Mir*. *Mir* had six docking ports on its core, plus some on the modules that were fixed to it.

The first American space station, *Skylab*, launched on May 14, 1973. It carried special **telescopes** for studying Earth, the Sun, and other stars.

The astronauts who lived on *Skylab* arrived in an Apollo spacecraft. Because part of *Skylab* had broken during its launch, the first crew spent most of their time fixing it. They stayed 28 days.

Two more crews would go up to *Skylab*. The third crew spent 83 days in space. The astronauts studied what happens to people's bodies in space and did 300 experiments. In 1979, *Skylab* started falling back to Earth and broke apart.

Skylab is shown here in 1974. After eating, sleeping, and their other off-duty activities, astronauts on the three manned *Skylab* missions spent most of their time studying the Sun.

11

After *Salyut 1*, the Soviets built four more space stations. None of them lasted long. Then, in 1977, they launched *Salyut 6*. This space station was special because it had a second docking port. This meant that other spacecraft could bring the astronauts new supplies while they lived and worked there. *Salyut 6* and its crews could therefore stay in space longer.

Salyut 6 worked for nearly five years and was home to 16 crews. The crews sometimes stayed in orbit for months. In 1982, the Soviets launched *Salyut 7*. Missions to *Salyut 7* lasted for up to eight months.

Here we see generals Thomas Stafford (left) and Andriyan Nikolayev working on a training mission in 1972. Stafford docked with *Salyut 4* in 1975.

Mir means "peace" in Russian. The Soviet Union launched the Mir space station in 1986. Mir's core was based on Salyut 6's, but it had six docking ports instead of two. This meant that new modules could be added to the space station over time.

Laboratories, washrooms, and special cameras were some of the modules added. Mir weighed 20.4 tons (18.5 t) when it was launched. It weighed 130 tons (118 t) with all the new modules.

In 1991, the Soviet Union broke apart. Mir was still working in orbit, and Russia took it over. Mir spent 15 years in orbit. Nearly 100 astronauts visited this space station.

This is *Mir* as it looked in 1995, during a visit by the U.S. space shuttle *Atlantis*. *Mir* was finished in 1996, and the station was brought down in 2001.

Many of the missions to *Mir* were spent bringing new modules and adding them to the space station. It took 10 years to finish building *Mir*.

In January 1994, an astronaut on a mission called Soyuz TM18 set a record for the longest time a human spent in orbit. He stayed on *Mir* for 437 days. This helped scientists learn more about how space changes the human body.

On June 27, 1995, the U.S. **space shuttle** *Atlantis* flew to *Mir* with two Russians on board. This was the first **cooperative** flight between the United States and Russia.

Here the *Mir* crew poses with the U.S. crew of *Atlantis* in 1995. This was the first time an American shuttle had docked with the Russian station.

The International Space Station, or ISS, is the largest object people have ever sent into orbit. When it is finished, it will be even larger! Sixteen countries, including the United States, Russia, Japan, Brazil, and France, have been working together to build the ISS.

When it is complete, the International Space Station will have six different laboratories. Crews will test how different living things handle being in space. They will study distant **planets** and stars. They will also use the ISS to study Earth.

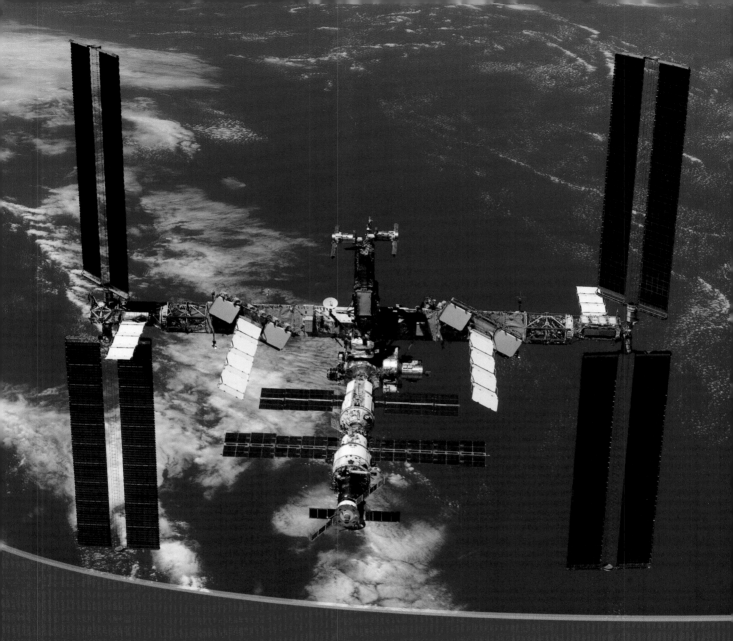

When finished, the ISS will be 356 feet (108.5 m) wide and 290 feet (88 m) long. It will fly over 85 percent of Earth.

The first two modules of the International Space Station were launched in 1998. On October 31, 2000, the first crews arrived to live on the space station. In 2008, crews brought up the largest module for the ISS. It was a laboratory from Japan, called Kibo. It was the size of a bus.

Building a space station while in orbit is risky work. Astronauts often have to do space walks to put the different pieces together. This means they are out in space, with only a space suit to keep them safe. Overall, it will take 46 missions to bring all of the pieces of the ISS into orbit.

Astronaut Joseph Tanner floats in space as he works on the ISS in 2006. He made two space walks, spending over 13 hours in space, to add parts to the station.

The crews living and working on the space stations have been studying how living in space for a long time changes the human body. They have also tried growing plants to see if people can produce their own food in space. One day, people may be able to visit the ISS and see what it is like to wake up in space.

What we learn on the ISS could also help us learn how to safely travel to other planets, such as Mars. The ISS may even help launch spacecraft to other planets. The possibilities are out of this world!

GLOSSARY

ASTRONAUTS (AS-truh-nots) People who are trained to travel in outer space.

COOPERATIVE (koh-AH-per-ah-tiv) Working with others.

EXPERIMENTS (ik-SPER-uh-ments) Tests done on something to learn more about it.

LABORATORY (LA-bruh-tor-ee) A room in which scientists do tests.

LAUNCHED (LONCHD) Pushed out or put into the air.

MISSION (MIH-shun) A special job.

PLANETS (PLA-nets) Large objects, such as Earth, that move around the Sun.

SATELLITE (SA-tih-lyt) A spacecraft that circles Earth.

SOVIET UNION (SOH-vee-et YOON-yun) A former country that reached from eastern Europe across Asia to the Pacific Ocean.

SPACE SHUTTLE (SPAYS SHUH-tul) A reusable spacecraft made to carry people and goods to and from space.

TELESCOPES (TEH-leh-skohps) Tools used to make faraway objects appear closer and larger.

INDEX

WEB SITES

Due to the changing nature of Internet links, PowerKids Press has developed an online list of Web sites related to the subject of this book. This site is updated regularly. Please use this link to access the list:
www.powerkidslinks.com/blastoff/stations/